Silver Burdett Picture Histories

Ancient Egyptians

Pierre Miquel
Illustrated by Pierre Probst

Translated by Eva Krauss
from La Vie privée des Hommes: Au temps des Anciens Egyptiens
first published in France in 1979 by
Librairie Hachette, Paris

© Librairie Hachette, 1979. Adapted and published in the
United States by Silver Burdett Company, Morristown, N.J. 1985 Printing.

ISBN 0-382-06585-9 (lib. bdg.)
ISBN 0-382-06926-9
Library of Congress Catalog Card No. 80-54636

Contents

In the Kingdom of the Gods

Long ago, Egypt was called the "Black Land." And in contrast to the ochre-colored earth of the plateaus and the pale sands of the deserts, the valley of the Nile, enriched by the silt washing down from the interior of Africa, did indeed seem very dark.

A FERTILE VALLEY

The plain of the Nile was extraordinarily rich. Each year, when the level of the river fell, it was necessary to quickly cultivate the fertile silt that had been left behind. The first farmers worked constantly from November to May. The peasants came down from their villages and repaired the dams and canals which allowed them to irrigate the land during the dry season. They reaped the abundant harvests which filled Egypt's first immense granaries.

Settling in this fertile valley, the farmers learned to push the ferocious crocodiles back from the shores of the river; to control the desert serpents; to domesticate cattle, sheep, and, later, horses. From the first cataract of the Nile to its delta, a distance of about 850 kilometers, the luxuriant valley sheltered the first organized political communities in the world. Egypt entered into history at the beginning of the third millenium B.C., when a legendary chief, the "pharaoh" Menes, is said to have brought under his rule the entire fertile valley, uniting under his authority the provinces of Lower Egypt in the north and Upper Egypt in the south. Menes is said to have reigned at Memphis, the capital of the two countries.

The pharaoh was considered a sort of living god whose exalted deeds were recorded in writing. The Egyptians wrote in characters called hieroglyphics, which modern men were not able to read until 1822.

3,000 years of history before Jesus Christ

Around 3000 B.C., unification of Egypt

OLD KINGDOM (2800-2300 B.C.)
- *The capital was Memphis.*
- *The pharaohs had gigantic tombs built for themselves—the pyramids.*

MIDDLE KINGDOM (2050-1650 B.C.)

After a period of unrest:
- *Thebes was the new capital.*
- *Expeditions left for the south.*
- *The Hyksos invaded the delta from the north.*

NEW KINGDOM (1550-1100 B.C.)
- *The pharaohs extended the empire north and south. Some of the most famous rulers were Ramses II and Amenophis IV and his wife Nefertiti.*
- *The famous monuments of Luxor and Karnak were built, as well as the fabulous treasure-filled tombs like that of Tutankhamen.*

Then Egypt became dominated successively by the Persians, Greeks, and Romans. The population of Egypt during the reign of Amenophis III of the New Kingdom is estimated at 9 or 10 million inhabitants.

From 2800 B.C. to 2300 B.C., the pharaohs of the Old Kingdom reigned over a prosperous land, protected from invasion by the desert peoples. They commissioned sculptors to make statues of them, and they directed the building of giant tombs—the famous pyramids. The pharaohs had at their command doctors, architects, priests, and, naturally, civil officers in charge of garnering the wheat and equipping the armies. One of the pharaohs, Pepi II, is believed to have reigned peacefully for 94 years. Time was already counted in years of 365 days, thanks to the scientific knowledge of their astronomers.

CONQUEST OF THE EMPIRE

The great Pepi II made the mistake of putting too much confidence in his officials, who then came to believe that they were independent in their own provinces. After Pepi's death, there was a long period of unrest, which destroyed the peaceful unity of Egypt. The rulers stole their neighbors' lands and imposed heavy burdens on the poor peasants, forcing them to make war and destroy crops. Two cities, however, succeeded in maintaining order around them—Heracleopolis and Thebes. Thebes, a city of Upper Egypt, was finally the victor and reunited the country. The Middle Kingdom lasted from 2050 B.C. to 1650 B.C. The new pharaohs of Thebes imposed on the country the worship of the god Amon, whom they associated with the ancient sun god of the first Egyptians. The new pharaohs built temples and magnificent tombs. In the east, they constructed a great fortified wall to protect themselves from invasion from Asia. They undertook to dry out the swamps of the Fayum, southwest of Memphis, thus acquiring more than 10,000 acres for cultivation. So much rich land was bound to tempt invaders. The Hyksos attacked and conquered Egypt, and once again, the Empire was subject to pillage.

The Hyksos, who came from Asia, possessed formidable war chariots, harnessed to horses, which were as yet unknown in Egypt, and they spread terror throughout the land. However, these hordes were driven out by a pharaoh of Thebes named

The obelisks

— *The Egyptian obelisks are tall stones cut from a single block of granite.*
— *They were often placed in pairs in front of temples.*
— *On their surfaces, engraved in hieroglyphics, are the names of the rulers who had ordered them made.*
— *At Karnak, the two obelisks of Queen Hatshepsut weigh about 320 tons and are 29 meters high.*
— *The obelisk on the Place de la Concorde in Paris comes from Luxor; those in London and New York, from Heliopolis.*

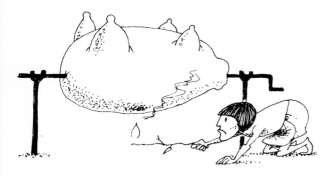

Kamose, and in 1580 B.C., the citadel of the Hyksos was taken by force, and the New Kingdom began.

A FRAGILE UNITY

From 1550 B.C. to 1100 B.C., Egypt enjoyed its third long period of unity. The new pharaohs engaged in a policy of conquest. They were so successful that the Egyptians became the masters of Palestine and Syria. They went up the Nile and conquered Nubia, and eventually they dominated the entire Mideast. But in order to maintain their position, they had to constantly impose their authority in Asia. The army was always on the march and its expeditions cost the state a fortune. The mines of Asia and of the deserts east of the Nile and the development of commerce, especially with Nubia, which was rich in gold, enabled the pharaohs to enlarge their cities, build temples, and attract to their court artists of great renown. The magnificent temples of Luxor and Karnak date from this period. To maintain their position, the pharaohs Tutankhamen, Seti, and Ramses II had to battle long and hard against powerful adversaries such as the Hittites, who came from Asia Minor and knew the metallurgy of iron. The last great pharaoh, Ramses II, was forced to give up Palestine.

From 1050 B.C. to 525 B.C., Egypt was unable to regain its former power. Divided politically, it once again became the prey of powerful invaders such as the Assyrians, who seized Memphis and Thebes; the Persians, who conquered the entire country; and then the Greeks. The Romans under Caesar established themselves with very little difficulty in Egypt, which was then governed by the famous Cleopatra.

ISIS AND OSIRIS

The Egyptians built one of the most brilliant civilizations in the history of humanity. The people worshipped many gods, who varied according to the region and the period. Certain gods, such as Ra, the sun god, and Nut, the sky goddess, became more important than others. Many of them evolved from the imagination of the people living in the countryside. One such god was Thueris, who had the body of a hippopotamus and the jaws of a crocodile. Another was Horus, the falcon god, the deity of one of the most ancient cults of Egypt. Osiris was believed to be a beneficent god, who was murdered by his brother Seth. Saved by his sister Isis, who restored him to life, Osiris became the god of the dead. The universal gods, such as Ra and Amon, were believed to be stern judges. Their priests wielded such power that they sometimes could threaten even the pharaohs.

The state lavished fortunes on the constant care of the temples where the gods were supposed to live. The priests had to perpetually maintain the rituals. Each morning the grand priest came to rouse the statue of the god by embracing it. The statue was then washed and dressed and given food. Lay people were not allowed to approach the statue except on great ceremonial days. On certain important days, the statue of Amon was carried to the Nile and placed in a boat for a ride on the river.

The Egyptians believed that the dead did not really die but would live on if care was taken to embalm their bodies and place them in their tombs, with food and other objects beside them. Entombed with them was the *Book of the Dead,* which contained formulas designed to save the soul on its journey to the other world.

ABSOLUTE POWER OF THE PHARAOH

Son of gods, interpreter of gods, a god himself, the pharaoh reigned over Egypt. He was to be worshipped not only while he lived, but since he was thought to be immortal, when enclosed in his tomb. Responsible for order, he regulated the labor of the peasants, rendered justice, waged war, and declared peace. He ruled with an iron hand over the viziers, governors, and scribes who represented his authority. An indiscreet official could receive a terrible punishment—his nose and ears might be cut off!

The family of the pharaoh might be very large because he had several wives. All the men and women of his kingdom belonged to the pharaoh. The one and only owner of land, goods, and animals, he lived off the labor of hundreds of thousands of peasants, who owed everything to him. By giving them land, as well as peasants to cultivate that land, he thanked his officials, soldiers, and friends. How-

Bread and beer

Bread
- *Most often prepared from barley flour, it was the basic food of the Egyptian people.*
- *One man generally consumed ten loaves of bread and two jugs of beer a day.*

  Different kinds of bread
- *soft, flat cakes*
- *hard, flat cakes*
- *hollow rolls (to be filled with vegetables)*
- *heavy, unleavened breads*
- *round, crusty breads*

Beer
Beer was made of bread crumbs and water sweetened with dates and left to ferment.

ever, they did not have the right to bequeath these gifts to their heirs without the pharaoh's permission.

Mines, quarries, and foreign commerce all depended directly on him. His granaries held the grain reserves of the entire country. The ones who benefited the most from the regime were the pharaoh's important servants—the nobles who commanded the army, the officials who directed the administration, and finally, the priests, who were always privileged.

BUILDING FOR ETERNITY

Peasants sometimes managed to acquire some education or to use their talents in activities involving the arts or crafts. Scribes often came from a rural background; the jewelers, goldsmiths, painters, and architects who resided in the courts of the pharaohs came from the common people, when they did not come from foreign lands. The Egyptians had excellent doctors. Some of them knew how to do such delicate operations as trepanation, which is the opening of the skull. Egypt's power attracted to it the most famous men in all the arts. Poets and storytellers used the 6,000 hieroglyphics of the Egyptian alphabet to recount on stone or papyrus the fates of the pharaohs or the life of the gods. The great pyramids and the many monuments attest to the Egyptians' mastery of mathematics as well as to the quality of a civilization which devoted considerable energy to building for eternity. This wish for immortality made Egypt a permanent museum of the early days of mankind's history.

In the tomb of Tutankhamen

- *chairs*
- *a gold and silver throne*
- *several beds*
- *trunks of clothes*
- *sandals and gloves*
- *vases and statues*
- *dishes*
- *baskets of food*
- *jugs of wine*
- *jars of ointments*
- *ornamental boxes*
- *jewelry*
- *gold and silver canes*
- *scepters*
- *lamps*
- *a fly swatter with ostrich plumes*

Land emerges from water

The farmers have come to the delta early in the morning to sow the wheat before the oppressive heat of the day. They must work quickly, for it is mid-October, and the great river has just receded. For four months, the land around the river was flooded. Now there is a layer of rich black silt. The earth is still soft and can easily be turned over. Now when the waters of the Nile still moisten the earth, the time is just right for sowing. But in a few days, the soil will dry and harden, and it will be more difficult to work.

As soon as the flood water drains off the land, oxen are hurriedly yoked to wooden plows and almost everyone in the villages leaves to work in the fields. The heavy soil is quickly broken up with hand tools or with the ox-drawn plows. The men with hoes and the sowers work together, preparing the soil and sowing the seed. Each sower takes the seeds from a reed basket which he has made himself. There is no need to cover the seeds to prevent the birds from eating them. The sheep and cattle which follow closely after the planters trample the seeds well into the rich dark soil.

When the harvest is ready, the scribes and agents of the landowners will measure the grain to determine how much should be saved as seed for the next planting, how much must be given to the landowners—nobles, temple priests, or the pharaoh himself—and how much each worker might keep to feed himself and his family.

The first sheaves gathered are offered to the gods. The grain is then poured into granaries. Woe unto the man who tries to steal from the harvest! The scribes are watching closely.

Sowing time under the Old Kingdom

is the end of summer and the figs are ripe. They must be gathered
nd dried. The peasants don't have to work too hard because they
ave trained monkeys to help them. It is necessary, however, to train
he monkeys not to eat the entire harvest!

fter the grape harvest, the new wine is put into jugs which are
ghtly covered by clay caps. On each jug is an inscription which
ecords the date, the origin, and the quality of the production.
New Kingdom)

To the rhythm of a flute, these harvesters are cutting the ripe grain
with curved sickles. The wheat is packed into large nets that will be
loaded onto a boat waiting on the Nile. Children follow the reapers to
glean what remains behind.

This granary is a veritable vault. The scribe carefully supervises the
men who carry in the grain and pour it into holes in the granary roof.
The grain can be removed through doors in the side of the granary. Before storing, the grain had been crushed and winnowed.

his balancing apparatus called a shaduf is used to raise the water of
he Nile into irrigation canals. The pail is emptied by hand. The shaduf
s still used in Egypt today to irrigate gardens.

In the papyrus forests

As it receded, the Nile left on its shores large expanses of water which formed marshes. Forests of tall papyrus reeds, flowers, and other aquatic plants grew in these areas. The marshlands of the Nile became more important the closer they were to the sea.

Hunters and fishermen inhabited these regions and papyrus was one of their main resources. The stalks gathered by the people of the villages were used to build huts with open walls. Sometimes the openings between the reeds were filled in with mud to make more solid walls. Rope, baskets, mats, and cages were also made of papyrus.

The main occupation of the people of the marshland was fishing, and they made many efficient fishing boats from papyrus. Some of these boats were even fitted with masts. The people fished with a hook and line or a scoop. Sometimes they formed groups of twelve to seine—to fish with a huge net which they dragged through the water, trapping the fish and then pulling their catch to shore. They also used harpoons to fish and to attack the numerous hippopotamuses on the river banks.

Hunting also provided valuable resources, for birds were plentiful. To capture them alive, two nets would be stretched from one side of a pond to another and then quickly pulled down over the startled birds.

As a sport, the rich people hunted in the marshes with throwing sticks, which usually had the carved head of a serpent at one end. When they succeeded in bringing down their prey, they would send children and servants to get it immediately because wild cats and crocodiles might be lurking nearby waiting to snatch it for themselves. It was necessary to be constantly on guard when venturing onto the shores of the Nile.

Gathering papyrus in the marshes of the delta

These inhabitants of the marshland are fishing with nets and with hooks and lines. When a fish is hooked, they stun it with a club. The fishermen position themselves along the river among the clumps of papyrus to surprise the fish, their main food.

Once the fish are caught, they are prepared for preservation. They are split in two, cleaned, and then put in the sun to dry. Sometimes, giant fish are caught, so large that it takes two men to carry them, but their delicate flesh can feed an entire village.

In the evening when they return, fishermen and sailors relax by engaging in water jousts. Sometimes a veritable battle develops.

In the foreground is a fisherman returning with his catch. He has also captured some water birds.

The large papyrus is the primary material for building the light, silent boats of these fishermen. The papyrus must be pulled together very tightly to be sure that the frail boats are waterproof. These boats do not last very long, but they can easily be replaced because of the limitless supply of papyrus.

The water lilies are blossoming. Along with the papyrus and the blue and white lotus, they beautify the shores of the Nile. Young girls are picking the flowers which are needed to decorate the temples and houses. Perhaps they will be used to adorn the table of the master who, in the background, is taking a ride in his comfortable boat.

Guardians of the herds

The herds of livestock belonging to the temples were countless. The temple of the god Amon possessed more than 400,000 heads of livestock; the temple of Ra at Heliopolis had almost 50,000. The temples in Egypt were the principal landowners, along with the princes of the reigning family, various dignitaries, and naturally, the pharaoh himself.

On a fixed date, the peasants were obliged to present the herds so that they could be counted and registered. All the domestic animals were brought to the courtyard of the estate, into the presence of the estate stewards. The animals were examined and their condition judged. The numbers of calves and lambs born within the year were carefully noted.

Since the beginning of their history, the Egyptians had domesticated dogs, valuable helpers for hunting. Oxen and donkeys were used for transportation; and cows, which were poor milk producers, were used to draw plows. Sheep were mainly appre-

ciated by the desert people. On the plain, pigs and goats were preferred. Milk, which was procured from goats, was made into cheese.

Chickens and horses, which came from Asia, appeared later. The horses were harnessed to war chariots in the era of Ramses II, but they were hardly ever ridden. Mounted soldiers did not appear until the arrival of the Assyrians in the beginning of the first millenium B.C.

The raising of livestock provided the tables of the rich with abundant and succulent meats. But the poor peasants, who were responsible for the herds, rarely benefitted from them.

Since it was entirely cultivated, the plain of the Nile could not be used for raising livestock. Only great estates had the facilities to maintain these important herds.

Presentation and registering of livestock

14

The first Egyptians tried to domesticate the desert animals. They were not successful with the oryx (foreground) nor the ibex. But they continued to try for a long time to raise them, fattening them by feeding them pellets of food.

The theft of livestock was very common on the farms. In an effort to prevent these thefts, the owners had their animals branded. They were lassoed and their front and back legs tied together. Then they were branded with a hot iron. The scribes carefully counted them.

The meat of geese and ducks was much enjoyed in Egypt. It constituted an important source of food for the people of the villages. Here they are being fed with grain. Grey cranes (foreground), which were captured on the banks of the river, were also raised.

These men must work hard to get their herd across the river safely. Since the little calves could easily drown, they must be tied to the boats. The ferryman uses a boat hook to keep the crocodiles away.

The herdsmen also utter magic words which were thought to render the crocodiles harmless. The herdsman who will watch over the flock at night has a mat tied over his shoulder.

Skillful craftsmen

These men are not free. Under the surveillance of a labor chief, they are constructing the surrounding walls of a temple. Prisoners of war who have become slaves, they came from Nubia or Palestine. The work is not difficult, but it is tedious. The men mix the mud of the Nile with chopped straw. They mold bricks which, once they are dried in the sun, become very durable. The temple itself will be constructed of stone or brick.

While slaves were used as laborers in ancient Egypt, there were relatively few of them, and most of the skilled craftsmen were free men.

The great estates were centers which brought together a great variety of craftsmen to work for the landowners. Among the highly skilled workers were bakers, weavers, carpenters, shipbuilders, bronze workers, shoemakers, and potters. The latter vied with each other to see who could make the cleverest and most daring shapes.

Usually the workers lacked for nothing. They were fed well from the estate's food reserves and were comfortably housed. Since money did not exist, they were paid a salary in goods. Sometimes, however, their situation became degrading. Then the workers would rebel and even go on strike. Sometimes they would appeal to the pharaoh and beg him not to let them die of hunger.

Some free men practiced their trades in the cities. Hairdressers, for example, set up their shops in the public squares, where they awaited their customers. Also along the city streets were bakers, shoemakers, and vendors of many different perfumes and spices.

Construction site of the surrounding wall of a temple built on a bank of the great Nile

...per was made from the pith of the papyrus plant which was cut into ...ips and placed in two alternating layers. The layers were then ...oistened and hammered until they formed a single layer which, ...sted to about 20 others, made up a papyrus scroll.

Egyptian spinners were very skillful. Above, a spinner is handling two spindles at once. The weavers are using a rudimentary loom placed horizontally. The Egyptians wove remarkable fabrics on these simple looms. (Old and Middle Kingdoms)

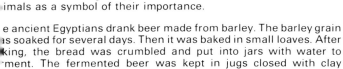

...e shoemakers know how to make sandals out of very fine calf's ...ather. The soles might be made from braided papyrus. Beginning ...th the Middle Kingdom, priests sometimes wore the skins of wild ...imals as a symbol of their importance.

...e ancient Egyptians drank beer made from barley. The barley grain ...s soaked for several days. Then it was baked in small loaves. After ...king, the bread was crumbled and put into jars with water to ...rment. The fermented beer was kept in jugs closed with clay

All Egyptian boats were not made of reeds! These carpenters are sawing thick planks of wood, assembling the parts of a boat, and using an adze to hollow out the prow, made from a tree trunk. They use hammers, chisels, small axes, and axes with long handles.

stoppers. In the right foreground, a woman prepares clay containers. In the background, the new beer is being poured into jars. In the left foreground, a brewer strains the fermented liquid through a basket-work sieve placed over a clay vat.

All metals are valuable

Gold was very valuable and was moved only under close watch. When it was delivered in rings or fine powder, the scribes registered it according to weight. The gold came from the desert separating the Nile from the Red Sea. It traveled in donkey caravans escorted by archers to guard against pillage by the Bedouins. In the mines, wells were dug and cisterns built so that the workers would not die of thirst. No one had the right to commandeer or assay the gold, which was considered the "flesh of the gods." Those who worked in the corridors of the mines were hardly able to see the gold. In the stifling darkness, the miners warmed the rock so that it would crumble more easily, before they started to work on it by driving wedges into the veins of precious metal.

Soon the mines in the desert were not enough, so the Egyptians started going up the Nile as far as the second cataract and began to exploit the mines of Nubia. They also searched for copper and precious stones in the Sinai. Weapons and tools were fashioned from bronze, a combination of copper and tin. The Egyptians did not learn how to make iron until the first millenium B.C.

The metallurgy workshops belonged to the temples or to the state. Gold and silver were used by goldsmiths and sculptors. Copper was employed by the makers of bronze tools and weapons, but sculptors also used this metal to make beautiful vases or temple gates. The arms makers and carriage makers covered war chariots with sheets of metal. The bronze workers were always under the supervision of overseers.

For a long time, farmers had only stone-edged sickles and soldiers had only spears with stone points. Since metals were rare and costly, they emerged very slowly into daily life.

Gold arrives at a goldsmith's shop and the gold rings are weighed.

A furnace for melting copper is built with circular bricks which retain heat. The melted copper settles to the bottom and the gangue, or mineral wastes, which remain on the surface, run down into a shallow basin. At right is a piece of copper and a ring of gangue.

These men are prisoners sentenced to work in the mines. They extract gold-bearing ore from the rocks. Children (background) bring the ore to the surface where it is crushed; the gold is refined and sent to the storehouses of the pharaoh, owner of all the mines.

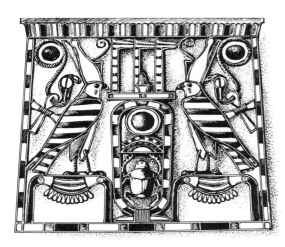

The Egyptians vigorously searched for beds of precious stones which were to be found in the desert. Their jewelers skillfully worked these stones into marvelous pieces of art. This breastplate is made of gold incrusted with lapis lazuli, carnelians, and turquoise.

These goldsmiths have made a sarcophagus. Now, they are going to apply a layer of gold leaf, molding it to the form with a bone, then polishing it with an agate. The image of the pharaoh must be resplendent. Nothing is too beautiful for the god in the form of man.

Inside this giant clay mold is the hollow form of a gate designed for a temple. On top of the mold are a number of little cups. Into these, the melters pour melted metal in successive layers. The gases escape

and the metal takes its shape. Powerful bellows activated continuously by the workers assure the melting of the large copper ingots whose shapes resemble animal skins.

Artists are everywhere

In the pink granite quarries of Aswan, an immense block has been found, which has given the sculptors the opportunity to form, from a single piece of granite, the colossal statue of a pharaoh. The work is almost finished. The artists are working on the last details under the vigilant eyes of their supervisor. With their bronze chisels and hard stone tools, they are carving out the last pleats of the loincloth. The polishers will finish the work.

To transport the granite statue to the temple, an army of men goes into action. First, they will place the statue on a gigantic sledge made of thick planks held together by cross-pieces. The men will then use four long ropes to drag the planks over the ground which has been made slippery by water bearers who keep it well sprinkled. A huge crowd will attend the departure of the statue, which is enveloped in incense and perfumes.

The quarries furnished the stone workers with very varied materials—red quartz; pink, gray, and black granite; alabaster; and a gritty, dark-hued shale. White limestone from south of Thebes was much sought after because it is easy to work.

The palaces, temples, and funeral monuments were matters of great concern to the pharaohs. They supported numerous craftsmen—stonecutters, architects, sculptors, painters, and bronzeworkers. Many of the workshops made luxury objects for the rich.

The stone sculptors competed with the sculptors in wood and bronze. The goldsmiths often enriched the statues with gold and precious stones, while painters decorated the tombs and palaces with frescoes whose colors have remained bright to this day.

The huge statue of a pharaoh

20

he making of stone vases is an Egyptian speciality. Here the drilling
strument is weighted with stones so that it will operate evenly and
roduce a symmetrical shape. Amphoras, goblets, bowls, and basins
ere made in this way. (Old Kingdom)

hese objects give us an idea of the sophistication of the artists. From
ft to right are a faience funerary statuette, a golden falcon's head,
nd an alabaster goblet. Above them is a makeup holder of wood and
ory, which represents a swimmer following a duck.

Since the Middle Kingdom, sculptors carved reliefs, cutting deep into
the stone. Here the artist is working the block of stone with a chisel,
according to a drawing already marked on the stone, carefully
following its outline. The stone is then polished.

The tomb painters are at work decorating a royal tomb. First they
make a drawing on a small piece of stone (foreground). Then they
reproduce it on the wall on a larger scale. On the stairway, an
assistant is grinding the cakes of color into powder.

his cabinetmaker has already made the frame for a rush-bottomed
hair. He is drilling holes in the wood through which reeds will be
hreaded. He is using an unusual drill, which is set in motion by a sort
f bow. Behind the cabinetmaker can be seen a tool box.

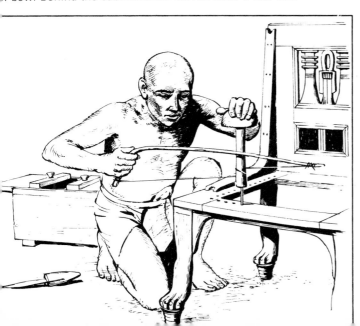

Cities and villages

Cities were rare in ancient Egypt. Rural society lived mainly in villages, which were centers for meeting and trading. The peasants did not travel around very much. Instead, in the village square on regular dates, they met merchants who supplied them with everything they needed.

Only the rich were able to buy luxury goods. Such a one is the dignitary of the Old Kingdom pictured above traveling in his litter. He carries his staff, the symbol of his authority, and is accompanied by his pet animals, a dog and a monkey. His servants are carrying his personal articles in a small chest.

If a village was not built on the banks of the river itself, it was established around some source of water. The houses of the inhabitants were mainly of brick or dried mud. In the marshlands, they were made of papyrus.

In the cities, the most important space was occupied by palaces and temples. The houses of the important dignitaries, surrounded by thick walls, sometimes covered more than an acre and had many luxuries, such as pools, gardens, and colonnaded galleries.

The merchants and craftsmen set up their wares in the busy streets where they made sandals, clothing, tools, and weapons. Certain streets emitted a repugnant odor—the street of the tanners, for example, because the animal skins were dried in the open air. In front of their shops, the potters offered their decorated wares to prospective buyers.

Within the shelter of thick brick walls, well protected behind heavy gates of bronze or thick wood, the city dwellers, like the villagers, lived without much contact with the outside world.

A dignitary is traveling by litter.

22

hen the river is high, the people of the village come to wash their ousehold linen. They twist the linen sheets to wring the water out of em and then they dry them on the white stones of the embankment. eanwhile the children fish in the river.

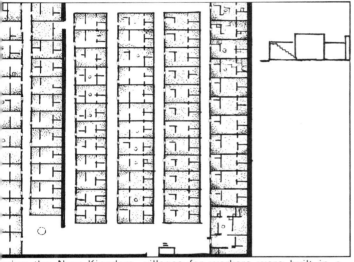

uring the New Kingdom, villages for workers were built in a eckerboard pattern and surrounded by a thick brick wall. The single ntrance gave access to a square with a well. Perpendicular roads parated the blocks of houses, each of which had four rooms, except e most important one, the foreman's (bottom right).

nce the ancient Egyptians did not use money, marketing was done barter. This merchant is offering salt (the two large slabs in the reground), wood, and willow reeds. In exchange, his customer

This barber has set up his shop under a canopy in the town square. The customers have a long wait. Some of them fall asleep; others play a game with dice. Once seated on the barber's three-legged stool, they have their heads washed with soapy water and their scalps shaved with a long razor.

offers him shell necklaces. In the background, a man is trading fruit for a rabbit.

The power of the scribes

A royal tomb in the Valley of the Kings has been robbed during the night. This is a serious affair. The vizier, chief minister of the pharaoh, has taken the trouble to come in person to question the suspects. The justice of the pharaoh knew no mercy. He possessed the power of life or death over his subjects. Was he not a god? Then how could he possibly make a mistake?

To obtain the truth from suspected thieves, torture was often used. First they were beaten on their backs, then on their feet and hands. Convicted thieves were subject to severe sentencing. For example, they might be sent to labor in the salt or gold mines. But if the judges themselves made a mistake, they might arouse the fury of the pharaoh who could have their noses or ears cut off.

The pharaoh governed Egypt with the help of high public officials, of whom the most important were the viziers. These viziers in turn commanded the important officials such as the governors of the provinces. The governors maintained justice and order; kept a police force; saw to the raising of an army, the collecting of taxes, and the supervision of great irrigation works and public building projects; all with the help of hosts of lesser officials such as overseers and the all-important scribes.

In a sense, the scribes were the true masters of the country. Their services were essential to the royal palace, the temples, and the army as well as to the smooth administration of government. They were educated in the temple schools and spent many years studying the complex, elaborate Egyptian system of writing. They had to be able to put on papyrus the texts of treaties, judiciary matters, and messages from the pharaoh, as well as the accounts of landowners. When they went into the government, they would often change services, going from the judiciary to the army, to important positions involving the maintenance of order in the towns.

Two men are accused of having pillaged a royal tomb and the vizier is conducting an inquiry.

"A boy's ears are on his back," say the scribes; "he listens when he is beaten." With stick in hand, this scribe is teaching hieroglyphics to the children. The students are practicing on stucco-coated tablets because papyrus is too costly for use in schools.

Below at left are hieroglyphics. At bottom, from top to bottom, a hieratic text is transcribed into hieroglyphics and then into the popular script. At right are the tools of a scribe—a palette, reed pens, inkwells, and a chest.

Peasants who cheat on the quantity of grain to be delivered to the agents of the pharaoh are severely punished. They can be subjected to dozens of whippings with a stick, receiving their punishment face down on the ground as the scribe looks on.

Conquered peoples are obliged to send the pharaoh a duly calculated annual tribute. These tributes—ivory shields, exotic animals, gold rings, precious stones—are registered by the officials of the vizier, and offered to the pharaoh with great ceremony.

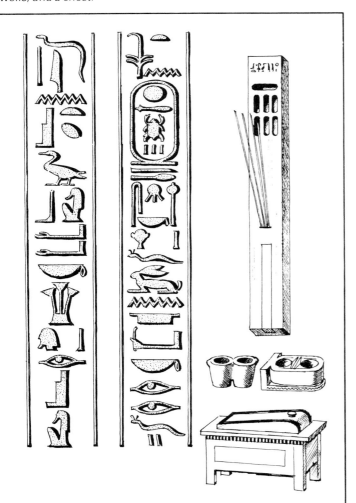

The pharaoh, a god on earth

The education of a pharaoh began at an early age. Very diligent instructors taught him the active sports, especially hunting, the sport of princes. He had to become a champion archer in order later on to chase and kill the gazelles of the desert from his speeding chariot.

The powers of the pharaoh were of a religious nature; he was adored as a divinity. His main function was to make certain that for the good of his kingdom, all the gods were satisfied. He also spent a great part of his time overseeing the maintenance and restoration of the temples and sanctuaries and the construction of new religious buildings, and personally practicing the adoration of the gods. A god himself, he possessed all the symbols of their supernatural power—the crook, the flail, and, on his head, the image of the cobra "uraeus."

In addition, he was responsible for the souls of his ancestors so that the order of nature would not be disturbed. The shining of the sun, the flooding of the Nile, and the coming of spring—all depended on the gods, so the pharaoh had to be a zealous priest. Master of the whole earth and owner of all Egypt, he meted out the duties for all the great work projects. He was responsible for irrigation, which he carefully regulated. He rendered justice according to the goddess Maat, who influenced him to either indulgence or severity.

The pharaoh had to be suspicious of everything. He constantly feared betrayal by the provincial governors who brought in the taxes and recruited soldiers for the army. Two grand viziers, responsible directly to the pharaoh, supervised the governors. But because the country was so long and the distance between the delta and the first cataract of the Nile so great, it was difficult to prevent intrigue.

The young prince is practicing archery.

Wearing the crown of Lower Egypt, the pharaoh is seated on his throne in all his majesty. He is receiving the crown of Upper Egypt from two priests who, in honor of this celebration, are dressed as the gods Horus (left) and Seth (right). (Middle Kingdom)

Crowns, scepters, and royal symbols. From left to right: the vulture and the cobra "uraeus," symbols of power (1, 2); the red crown of Lower Egypt, the white crown of Upper Egypt, and the double crown of Upper and Lower Egypt (3, 4, 5); the royal headdress with artificial

An official has earned the gratitude of the pharaoh, who appears with his wife and children at the window of the palace to give him his reward, a gold necklace. Some of these necklaces, fashioned in the royal workshops, weighed several kilograms. (New Kingdom)

beard worn on top of a wig (6, 7); the blue crown or *khepresch* (8); different forms of scepters: *aba* (9), *hedj* (10), *hega* (12), *ouas* (13), and the flail, *neheh* (11); the queen's crown with the vulture's skin of the XIXth Dynasty (14) and the queen's own scepter (15).

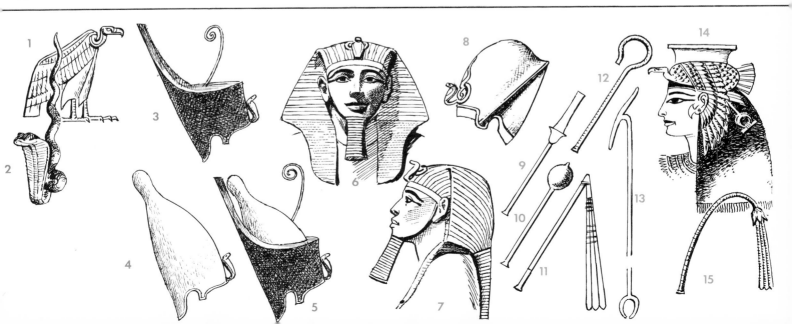

At home in ancient Egypt

Sheltered by a high brick wall, this rich man's home is hidden from public view. Inside their walls, the people delighted in caring for their trees and pet animals. On this dry and barren soil, the acacias, willows, date trees, pomegranate trees, and tamarisks had to be constantly watered. In the luxurious gardens pictured above, the family goose is quarreling with the mongoose who watches to make sure that snakes do not attack the children. Many wealthy people kept long-legged greyhounds, basset hounds, cats, and monkeys as pets.

Important people had slaves and servants in their houses. Although they were free men, the servants had to obey the orders of the master. They accompanied him when he went out, carrying his sandals for him, and making way for him in the street. The servants received and announced his visitors, and dressed him from head to foot. The women had maidservants to take care of the many children who were usually part of Egyptian families. Noblemen, who often had several wives, brought all their children up together. (The pharaoh Ramses II is said to have had 162 children!) In the less favored classes, the children were raised by their mother, who carried the newest infant in a pouch hung around her neck. When the children were no longer nursed, they were fed papyrus shoots and boiled roots. Many children died at an early age.

Children received a name which was registered by the scribes. The Egyptians did not have family names, and each child's name was different from his father's.

House and garden of a dignitary

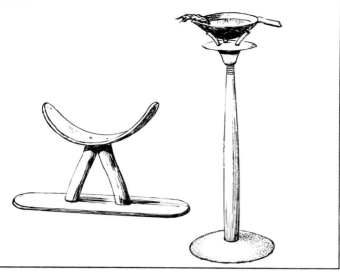

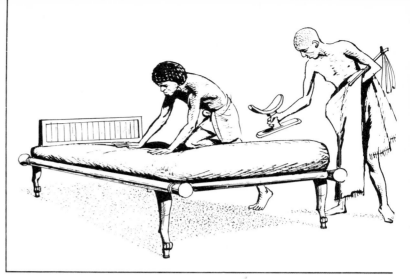

hese objects were part of the everyday life of the Egyptians. Even the oorest people slept with a headrest. The very simple one above elonged to a laborer. The oil lamp, placed on a stand in the form of a apyrus, was used to light the interior.

ch Egyptians were very fond of meats and poultry. In this kitchen of wealthy man, ducks and geese are being roasted on a spit. Beef and mb are cut into pieces before roasting. These roasts will be served th cabbage, onions, and cucumbers.

Two servants are preparing the bed of a rich Egyptian. One is spreading fresh sheets over some cushions. The other is going to put a fly chaser and a headrest on the wooden bed, which has only a footboard.

The lady of the house is being groomed. A handmaiden is combing the lady's hair and will then put on her makeup. The lady will be able to see the results in the mirror on the makeup chest. She is wearing an amulet around her neck to keep the evil spirits away.

Living close to nature

The Egyptians enjoyed many leisure activities. Children often got together to play one of their favorite games, "goat on the ground." Two boys would sit down on the ground, facing each other with their legs stretched out, while their friends had to jump over them without being caught. They also held knee races, running while holding their feet with their hands. The boys engaged in wrestling, hunting, and javelin or stone throwing. The girls got together to dance and be admired by the boys. The boys often played the flute while the girls swam, generally nude or dressed in light linen with a ribbon around their hair.

Often at the end of the family meal, a flute, lute, or small drum would be played. Among the rich, there might be harp or zither music. The Egyptians also got together in the evening to listen to storytellers narrate mysterious tales and recount ancient legends.

The young nobles accompanied their fathers in their favorite pastime—hunting in the desert. They pursued antelopes and gazelles with bows and arrows, and they searched for ostrich eggs and plumes. Their hunting experiences were a valuable way of training rich young men to be warriors for Egypt's armies.

The poorer village youths hunted with throwing sticks, and used nets to trap fish to provide food for themselves and their families.

So it was that in ancient Egypt both rich and poor lived very close to nature and partook of the simple joys of outdoor games and of fishing and hunting.

Swimming and music were two favorite diversions of the Egyptians.

Children of wealthy Egyptian families played with wooden toys cleverly made with movable joints. Toy models of crocodiles and hippopotamuses such as those shown above were the most popular. Dolls for little girls were made of wood or clay.

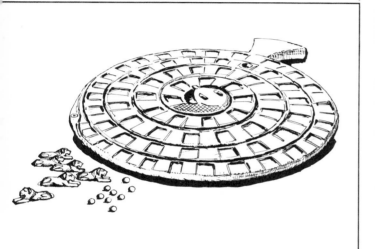

The oldest known game of the Egyptians is the game of the serpent. It was called this because the "board" was composed of a large number of squares arranged in a snake-like spiral. Each player moved forward three lions and three lionesses by throwing red and white marbles onto the squares and noting where they landed.

Physical exercise was encouraged in the schools. But the children, so numerous in Egypt, also played in the street or in the village square. At left, the boy crouching on the ground is supposed to guess who is

The pharaoh plays senit with a woman of his harem. It is a game like backgammon or checkers, played on a board with 33 squares. The pieces, black or white, are shaped like cones or spools. The game can last a very long time. The ordinary people of Egypt also enjoyed playing senit with their families.

hitting him. In the background, two boys are wrestling. Two other boys are exercising with dumbbells. The four young girls are playing ball in pairs.

Feasts and merrymaking

The governor is having a party! In his magnificent home with a terrace overlooking the Nile, he is receiving his guests from the province, lords of the noble families and government officials. The master of the house and his wife are seated side by side on low chairs. They are wearing their finest jewels on their elaborate clothing and will not leave their seats during the entire reception. In front of them, young musicians are playing the lute and the double flute.

The guests are seated on mats. Men and women form separate groups, with the former being served by young boys and the latter by young girls. The servants adorn the guests with garlands of flowers and constantly replace the cones of perfumed fat on top of the women's heads. They also massage the arms of both men and women with unguents and perfumes.

The feast is brought in—delicate fish cooked over fires of wood and aromatic plants, geese and ducks roasted on a spit, and skewers full of roasted birds. The servants offer baskets filled with figs, watermelon, and grapes. Many very sweet cakes are also served. Wine and beer are drunk as the guests eat dates, pomegranates, and fruits imported from Syria. The women and children sip a liqueur called grenadine, which is made from pomegranates.

After the meal, there will be a concert by harpists and flutists. Some musicians from Asia will play the five-stringed zither. The double flute and the lute were the most popular instruments for accompanying dancers and singers. Often, one of the guests thanked his host by improvising a sort of chanted poem accompanied by the musicians. They also thanked the gods, for all ceremonies, even family ones, had a religious aspect.

A party at the governor's

harpists, one of whom at the far right is blind, draw sad notes
m their instruments, which are shaped like shovels. It is a funeral

concert. The singers chant in cadence to the sound of the double flute
and the long flute made from reeds.

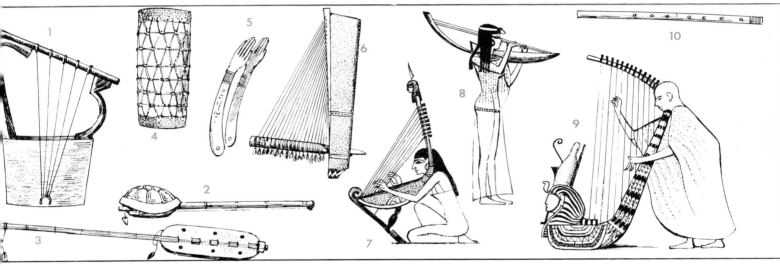

sical instruments of the Egyptians. From left to right: the zither (1);
lutes, one of which has a resonance case made of a turtle shell (2,
a drum (4); clappers in the form of the "Hand of Hathor" (5); various

harps—the angular harp with twenty-one or more strings (6), a harp
with a floor rest (7), a shoulder harp (8), the great ceremonial harp,
richly decorated (9); and finally, the reed flute (10).

the young girls of this village can dance. For the acrobatic dances,
y must learn to walk on their hands and do somersaults. In the
eground, a girl is playing a sestrum or timbrel, the handle of which
s a carving of the goddess Hathor.

The musical instruments which accompany the dancers are quite
simple. Sometimes the children themselves made their instruments,
such as these little lotus blossom-shaped clappers which they knock
against each other.

The secrets of hunting and fishing

Thanks to their ingenuity and cunning, the Egyptians were able to attack the large wild animals which menaced their environment. To rid the Nile of its hippopotamuses and crocodiles, the hunters employed a harpoon mounted on a wooden stick, which they plunged deeply into the jaw of the animal, breaking the handle like a piece of straw. But the hunters above have taken the precaution of tying the harpoon to a heavy rope equipped with buoys. Then, all they have to do is retrieve the rope and pull very hard to bring the animal within their reach so that they can finish it off with other harpoons. It is a very sporting hunt!

Sometimes the pharaoh undertook a long journey to go hunting. In the desert, he mainly hunted lions. He also hunted antelopes and gazelles, but ignored the hyenas. In general, the sovereign hunted alone in his chariot drawn by swift horses, and accompanied by his greyhounds.

The peasants had to get rid of the animals that destroyed their crops. Close to the trees, they spread out a huge, closely-woven net, the corners of which were secured by large stakes. The children hid in the branches and when the quail, orioles, and other small birds landed on the plants, they released the corners of the net, entangling the birds. Then they quickly slid underneath the net and gathered the surprised birds, like fruit.

The fishermen used several kinds of equipment, such as hooks and lines, nets, scoops, simple traps, or those with two compartments where the fish entered, attracted by the bait, but could not get out and so were captured alive. The fishermen also fished with nets in the marshlands. The fish were stunned with clubs after they were caught in the nets.

A hippopotamus hunt

34

vift Algerian greyhounds have chased the game into an enclosure rrounded by a net. Gazelles, antelopes, and hyenas are caught in e trap. The hunters have only to riddle them with arrows and finish em off with an axe or knife.

der the direction of a master fisherman, these men draw in the net ich they have placed quite a distance from the shore by means of ats. The fish, split open and gutted, will be dried in the sun and eserved by salting. This is the main food of the villagers.

This boat has silently slipped into the marsh, and the hunters have succeeded in surprising wild ducks, which they attack with a boomerang. The delta abounds with game. Some of the people subsist almost entirely by fishing and hunting.

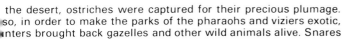

the desert, ostriches were captured for their precious plumage. so, in order to make the parks of the pharaohs and viziers exotic, nters brought back gazelles and other wild animals alive. Snares were set to trap the animals in pits covered with nets. Noblemen chased gazelles and wild bulls on their chariots, attacking them with bows and spears.

Heavy traffic on the Nile

Only the man at the helm is working; the rowers are at rest. Driven by the wind, the boat is going down the Nile on her return voyage from Nubia. The large rectangular sail, wider than it is high, is taking the crew toward the delta. A small monkey is also making the voyage.

At the prow, the pilot probes the riverbed with a pole in order to avoid any surprises, such as shifting sand banks or sharp rocks that would rip apart the fragile bark. When the wind dies, the rowers start to work, then the captain hoists himself up on top of the cabin to shout his orders. The cabin, in the center of the boat, provides a shelter where the voyagers can escape the implacable sun, and sleep. This type of boat sometimes had stalls for horses when it was transporting a nobleman who was on the way to the hunt, or soldiers on an expedition.

Convoys of merchant ships, loaded to the brim, constantly traveled on the Nile. Built of durable wood, these large flat-bottomed boats were big enough to transport colossal statues or blocks of marble. The crew ate on board, and in the cabins, an entire beef could be carved up and stored, along with jugs of beer. The ships were generally towed up the river.

Seagoing boats were able to reach the coasts of Somaliland and Syria, where the wood necessary for naval construction could be obtained. These boats had large oars in the stern which served as rudders, and a square sail with a single or double mast. To allow for passage of the boats, the pharaohs had a canal dug between the Red Sea and the Mediterranean.

The Egyptians fought very little at sea, their boats being used mainly for commerce or the transportation of troops.

Along the Nile

our types of Egyptian boats: 1) a supply ship for the transportation of vestock or crops; 2) a sailboat of the Old Kingdom, with square sail nd double mast; 3) a procession or pilgrimage boat of the New ingdom; 4) a boat, used for the transportation of statues and belisks, being towed by several small boats.

he pharaohs often sent boats to the coast of Syria to maintain lines f commerce or to launch military expeditions. When the sea was ery calm, as in this picture, the mast was lowered, the sail detached

Skins, ivory, myrrh trees, gold, and monkeys are being loaded on board a large trading ship in the Land of Punt on the coast of Somaliland. The boat is rigged with an enormous square sail, solidly affixed to a mast by four ropes. The big ship is manned by a crew of many rowers.

and folded, and the crew set to rowing. The eyes painted on the front of the ships were designed to protect against evil spirits.

Treasures of the desert

A Greek author once declared that Egypt was a gift of the Nile. Nothing could be more true. If the ancient Egyptians moved more than a few kilometers from the fertile river valley, they found themselves in the desert, which both isolated and protected Egypt from the rest of the world, and, particularly, from Asia. It was from Asia that the Bedouins came, attracted by the riches of the Nile Valley. These nomads, who were often starving, formed little caravans with their wives and children, their meager belongings loaded on the back of a mule, because the camel was as yet unknown. Great was their relief when they finally arrived at the boundary marking the Egyptian frontier. There they had to face the interrogation of Egyptian officials, but the people of the valley were usually quite gracious to the newcomers.

The Egyptians feared the desert, empire of the god Seth, who was for them a kind of evil demon.

From the desert came harsh sandstorms. It was also haunted by exotic, imaginary animals which struck terror to their hearts. However, this did not prevent the Egyptians from penetrating these fearsome wastelands, first to hunt lions and antelopes, but more importantly, to look for minerals. The state, owner of all the mines, maintained a desert police force to watch over them.

Following the Nile, the Egyptians also entered the desert regions of the south, near Nubia, the Sudan of today, where there were still gold mines. In the native villages, they managed to barter their wares for the products of the neighboring deserts or savannahs of the south, near the mysterious sources of the Nile.

Asiatic emigrants arrive at the Egyptian frontier, which is marked by a pillar.

out 3,400 years ago, Prince Thutmose stopped to sleep near a
amid. In his sleep, he heard the cries of the Great Sphinx,
npletely buried under the sand by the winds of the desert. When he
ame king, Thutmose had the giant statue uncovered.

thering honey in the desert. Mounted on a donkey, with a fly
aser in his hand, the master waits for the servants to take from the
heycombs the precious honey which was the only sweetener the
yptians had for their food.

An expedition has been organized to dig a well in the area of a mine in
the desert. The men, working under the protection of the desert
police, take the sand out in baskets, but they are still far from reach-
ing water.

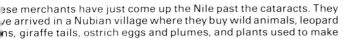

ese merchants have just come up the Nile past the cataracts. They
ve arrived in a Nubian village where they buy wild animals, leopard
ns, giraffe tails, ostrich eggs and plumes, and plants used to make

perfume. The people of Nubia happily welcome the merchants, who
pay them with cheap jewelry and cloth. Later the merchants will sell
their exotic goods for very high prices in the cities of Egypt.

The charioteers, an enviable army

These archers, who are dancing to the sound of a drum, are Nubians enlisted in the Egyptian army. When the pharaoh sends them into combat, he has them branded like cattle so they cannot escape. They receive very hard training in the Egyptian army. The officers do not tolerate any weakness. The poor soliders are punished by beatings.

The scribes went from village to village to recruit soldiers who were then assigned to the infantry, archery units, or to the chariot cavalry. In the latter case, they were under the orders of the horsemen and chariot masters, who were always aristocrats. Indeed, only the rich had the means to provide the very expensive chariot and the two swift horses which took it into battle. The horseman's duty was to handle the chariot while the warrior fired arrows and javelins at the enemy.

On the battlefield, the officers and the men carried arms, provisions, and water on their backs.

In addition, the pharaoh saw to it that his troops received provisions regularly. Reserves of meat, bread, cake, and vegetables were transported on wagons drawn by oxen. But very often the army had to live by pillaging.

Old soldiers could not become chariot masters, but the pharaoh treated them well. He granted them rewards—necklaces or pieces of gold. When they retired, he made them chiefs of the urban police or gave them houses and land. If they won a battle, the soldiers could profit from the spoils of the vanquished enemy. This hope for profit explains the large enrollments and why the Egyptian army never lacked for men.

War dance and battle practice of Nubian soldiers, who are part of the garrison of a fortress (Middle Kingdom)

The chief of the village is presenting the young men who are eligible for the army to the scribe sent by the governor of the province. The official will register them on the list of recruits. Those who are not in good physical condition will be rejected.

Egyptian soliders often had to cross deserts when they went on expedition. One of the leaders' jobs was to locate watering places so that their troops did not die of thirst while on the march. Here they have found an oasis in the desert.

One of the duties of the army was to assure the protection of the caravans such as the one above which is transporting gold taken from the mines. The Bedouin plunderers often attempted a surprise raid, and the pharaoh did not want to lose any of his gold.

The army served as laborers in big work projects. By the hundreds, the soldiers here are harnessed to a sledge which is transporting the colossal statue of a pharaoh to a new temple. The army also participated in the construction of important public works.

The chariot was the noble and envied weapon of the Egyptian army. The nobles, princes, and scribes fought on the chariots harnessed to horses. At night they slept in improvised camps, surrounded by

shields which formed a protective wall (extreme right). Here the soldiers are checking the condition of the chariot wheels, grooming the horses, and preparing their temporary quarters.

Woe to the vanquished soldiers!

The pharaoh always led the battle in person, advancing on his chariot, surrounded by his mercenaries. The infantry was heavily equipped, the soldiers carrying spears, shields, axes, and knapsacks. The infantry marched ahead of the rest of the army, the men advancing in eight parallel rows, one behind the other. The trumpeters, who followed them, gave the orders by blowing short blasts. Then came the corps of archers, and finally, the chariots.

Sometimes there were several hundred chariots in a battle. They were not very stable and easily turned over on the stony terrain, in which case the unskillful driver would be severely punished after the battle. If the accident happened in front of the enemy, the only salvation was to flee on the horses if there was time to unharness them.

The battle usually began with shots from the archers. Then came the charge of the charioteers with the pharaoh at their head. A skirmish of chariots then took place while the pikes of the infantry knocked against each other. Duels were fought with bent sabers. When the enemy was pushed back into a fortified place, the Egyptians began the siege, by riddling the defenders of the battlements with arrows. The ramparts, which were often made of wood, were approached and set on fire. Once the trenches were filled with all kinds of available material, the gates were battered down.

A victory was the occasion for great rejoicing. The sharing of the plunder was done systematically, under the control of the scribes. The pharaoh gave everyone a share. As for the vanquished, they had to give the pharaoh a determined amount of gold, silver, ivory shields, and a variety of other handmade objects.

Ramses II, preceded by his lion, charges against the Syrians.

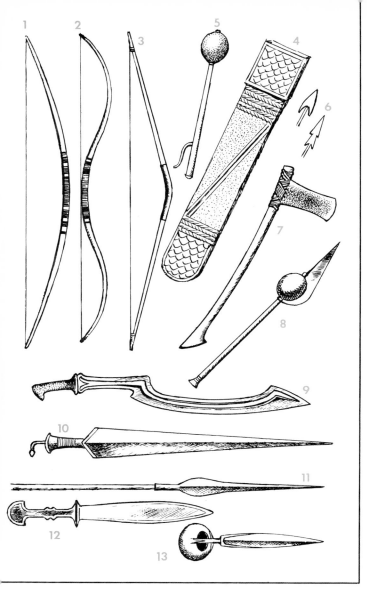

Weapons: various kinds of bows (1, 2, 3); a quiver (4); a club with a hand guard (5); arrowheads (6); an infantry combat axe (7); a club-knife (8); a bent or harp-shaped saber (9); a sword (10); a spear-head (11); daggers (12, 13)

After the victory, the number of enemies killed was counted by counting the right hands cut off the bodies. Here, the pharaoh, surrounded by his guards, listens to a scribe's report.

At the close of the battle, these prisoners are securely tied with ropes. They are lined up in long rows to be taken back to Egypt. The pharaoh's triumph will be extolled when he rides into the royal city of

Thebes. The prisoners will be forced to enter the army or work on the pharaoh's estates or those of the temples.

The gods on parade

During the flooding of the Nile, the Egyptians assembled by the hundreds of thousands in Thebes at the temple of the god Amon. Inside the sanctuary, the priests carried the divine statue on a model of a wooden boat, fitted at both ends with rams' heads. Another boat, decorated with the head of a woman, carried the statue of Mut, Amon's wife; and a third boat, distinguished by its falcon head, followed, bringing the statue of Khonsu, their son. In this way the gods left the temple, hidden in a tabernacle and carried by men with shaved heads. They were preceded by priests dressed in panther skins, who spread incense; and by standard-bearers and flag carriers.

On the shores of the Nile, the statues were hoisted onto real boats that were elaborately decorated. The statues were placed in a temple-like shelter constructed on the bridge, in front of which were placed obelisks and sphinxes. Armed soldiers towed the sacred boat into the river where it was made fast to a vessel manned by rowers. Thus, the god, followed by his wife and their son, went solemnly from Karnak to Luxor. Twenty-four days later, Amon resumed occupation of his own temple, accompanied by a huge crowd.

The pilgrims aboard the boats on the river sang sacred hymns and feasted and reveled. The girls danced and the merchants sold their wares. Then the peasants returned to their villages with the satisfied feeling of having done what was necessary to assure a fruitful year.

Thus, each god had his own festivals. Rich and poor always participated in these spectacular ceremonies.

Procession of Amon's bark through the temple. The face of the god is hidden from the eyes of the public.

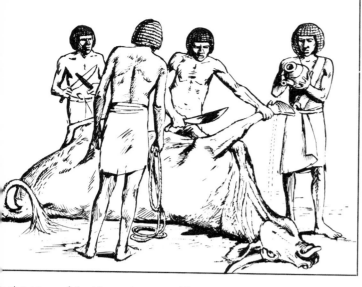

In the name of the king, priests sacrifice a bull on which they sprinkle a libation. These bloody sacrifices, performed at the time of funerals or certain festivals, were rare. Wild beasts were chosen, whose flesh was eaten with the hope of acquiring their strength.

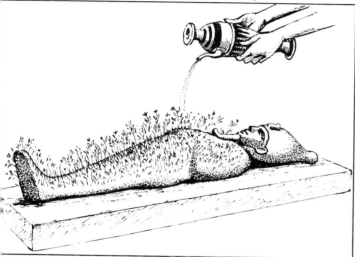

Osiris was assassinated by Seth. But his body, carried by the Nile, was found by Isis at Byblos. The cult of Osiris, god of life and of vegetation, was very popular. Figurines of the god were sprinkled with water in order to make the seeds grow.

The inhabitants of Memphis worshipped a bull-god named Hapi. There was always a real bull which had been carefully chosen at birth and introduced into the temple of the god Ptah. It was given enriched

This painted column is the pillar of Djed which was identified at the shrine of Osiris. Here with due ceremony, after several years of his reign, the pharaoh is raising the column. It was thought that this ceremony would magically regenerate his royal power.

food and treated with great care. Lavishly decorated, as in this picture, the bull was solemnly led through the entire village. At its death, it was embalmed and buried like a king in a sumptuous tomb.

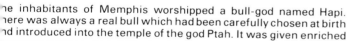

Extraordinary architects

In order to honor their gods and their pharaohs, the Egyptians wished to build indestructible temples and tombs. For this, enormous blocks of stones were needed. The search for these stones was sometimes conducted like a military expedition. Ramses IV mobilized almost 10,000 men to go in search of the stone of Bekhen. One of the grand priests of Amon accompanied him, surrounded by twenty scribes and a major general. More than 5,000 soldiers employed as laborers, large numbers of officials, priests, squires, and even fishermen charged with providing food for the troops were part of the expedition.

The blocks which would be used for the construction of the temple and the creation of the statues were carefully selected, and by sheer hard labor, 130 quarrymen and stone cutters detached the blocks one by one, and placed them in barges on the Nile. Later they were moved overland on large wood logs or sledges.

Besides temples and tombs, the Egyptians built luxurious palaces for the pharaohs and high dignitaries. These buildings were usually one story. In the center of the facade of the palace at El Amarna was the "balcony of the royal appearances." On the feast of Amon, the sovereign, accompanied by his queen, appeared on the balcony to show himself to the people. In front of the balcony were four richly decorated columns, shaped like papyrus, surmounting a ledge three stories high. The interior of the palace contained courtyards surrounded by columns, large halls with painted or sculptured columns, bedrooms, and bathing rooms. Spacious and beautiful gardens set off the palaces and mansions of the rich.

By piling up earth and building ramps, the blocks of stone could be put in place for the artists to paint and carve. The earth would then be gradually cleared away.

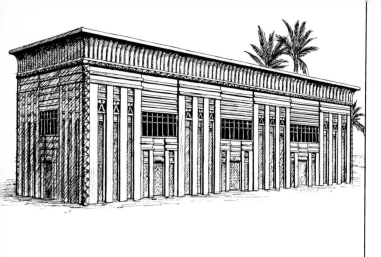

This house of the Old Kingdom is made of wood and reeds. Artfully decorated, it is composed of one solid framework. Later, when the houses were built of brick or stone, the Egyptians still kept the feeling of this primitive construction.

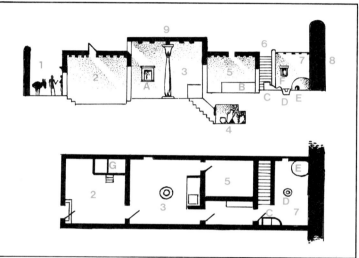

Plan of a home during the New Kingdom: 1) road; 2) outer room; 3) living room; 4) basement; 5) bedroom; 6) stairway to roof; 7) kitchen; 8) outside wall; 9) flat roofs; A) niche; B) couch; C) kneading trough; D) large container; E) oven; F) niche; G) bed or bench

Columns of Egyptian temples from left to right: the protodoric column, the palm column, the lotus column, the papyrus column, the bell column, and the hathoric column with a capital representing the head of the goddess Hathor, who had ears like a cow.

These pieces of Aswan granite have been pierced with holes into which have been wedged pieces of wood. When water is poured on the wood, it expands and the rock bursts. The workers could then detach blocks of stone and transport them to the construction site.

Five men are working on this block to give it the dimensions and the form desired by the architect. One of them measures the height; the others are checking parallelism. The roughness of the granite is smoothed away with a mallet and a chisel.

Giant tombs

The pyramids are gigantic tombs constructed by the Egyptians of the Old and Middle Kingdoms to shelter the bodies of the pharaohs and provide a place to worship them after their death. The Great Pyramid of Cheops can be reached by the Nile. Worshippers would arrive at a first temple built along the river. A covered gallery led to a second temple designed for the worship of the sovereign.

A monumental sphinx guards the three pyramids of Cheops, Chephren, and Mycerinus at Giza, not far from Memphis. They were erected for the pharaohs of the IVth Dynasty. Near the tomb of the kings, smaller pyramids contain the sarcophagi of the queens. There are about sixty of these pyramids in Upper and Lower Egypt.

Large expeditions were organized to transport on foot the millions of tons of stone which were extracted from the quarries. The pharaohs were not stingy about the costs. Their tombs were meant to be indestructible and inaccessible.

The proportions of the pyramids at Giza are notable. The pyramid of Cheops is 147 meters high and 227 meters from side to side. These blocks of stone were at one time covered with limestone and granite and had a smooth appearance. They were constructed by the use of ramps on which the material was drawn up. This required a tremendous amount of human labor.

The pyramids contained groups of funeral chambers ventilated by ducts. The sarcophagi of the kings and queens were placed in these chambers. The entrance to the gallery leading to the royal sarcophagus was kept secret at the time of construction, doubtlessly to discourage would-be robbers, but above all, to protect the repose of the soul of the king-god.

Under the New Kingdom, the pharaohs had themselves entombed to the west of Thebes in the Valley of the Kings. There, they constructed superb funeral temples, sometimes one hundred meters long and with religious decorations on the walls.

A great pyramid with its temple at the water's edge, its covered walkway, and funeral temple

In order to determine the direction of true north, before the construction of the pyramid, a perfectly horizontal circular wall was put up to create an artificial horizon. In the picture above a priest stands in the center of the circle and charts the rising and setting of a star by using a stake with a cleft at its upper end. North is exactly in the center of the two positions marked out on the wall by the assistant with a plumb line.

Cross section of the Great Pyramid of Cheops A) entrance; B) descending corridor opening into an unfinished vault; C) and D) ascending corridor and grand corridor opening into the first abandoned funeral chamber (E), and also into the king's room containing the sarcophagus (F); G) and H) ventilation ducts

Detail of the king's funeral chamber with sarcophagus (F); L) roof of the chamber, slabs and spaces providing for discharge of water from roof; F bis) antichamber of self-locking portcullises; D) entrance to the great ascending gallery; A) and B) another system of blocking off access to a corridor by sliding a movable block of stone.

The Egyptians lacked any kind of machinery for lifting or raising, so an enormous number of workers—peasants, soldiers, and prisoners of war—was needed for construction of the pyramids. Building materials were carried by barge on the Nile and then by foot to the building site. Ropes were used to pull the blocks of stone up ramps made of dirt and rubble.

In the holy of holies

There were more than 700 gods in the religion of the ancient Egyptians! Each region had its own gods and kept them even if they also adopted the more universal gods of the rest of the kingdom, such as Ra, the sun-god; Nut, the sky goddess; Amon-Ra, the god of Thebes; or Horus, the falcon-god. Many of these gods had animal aspects. The goddess Thueris had the body of a hippopotamus; Anubis, the head of a jackal. Others could turn themselves into animals, such as the bull, Apis, or the ram, Amon. These gods protected men against calamities. Thus, Horus drove away Seth, the desert wind; and Osiris promoted the growth of vegetation.

For each of these divinities, the pharaoh required a worship ritual. The main goal of this worship was to maintain order in the world. The Egyptians believed it was necessary to say prayers to assure that the balance of the seasons, planets, and forces of life and death be guaranteed by the gods.

Thus, catastrophes were avoided, and life and harmony maintained.

The temples were the dwelling places of the gods. They were built for them as were the palaces for the pharaohs. The role of the priest was to serve the gods from morning to night. Every morning, the grand priest of the sanctuary himself would go to awaken the god by singing his praises and blowing life into the statue, where the soul of the god reposed.

The priests received their education in the temples' "Houses of Life." These were a kind of school where the priests learned all the gestures, prayers, and sacred texts which were involved with the cult of each god. The priests were the professionals of Egyptian religion and the office was handed down from father to son.

Peasants bringing offerings to the temple

50

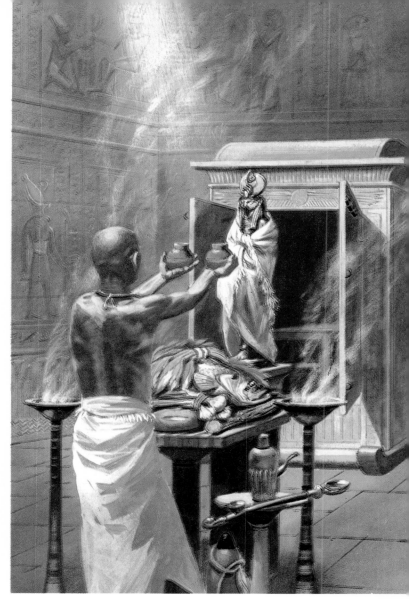

The level of the sacred lake of a temple varied according to the waters of the Nile. In this water, the priest above is performing ritual ablutions. By sprinkling himself with the water from the lake, he purifies himself.

This temple of Ramses II, at Abu Simbel (left), is dug deeply into the mountain. It contains an entrance with a seated statue (1) and a sanctuary (2). Twice a year, on October 19 and February 21, the rising sun penetrates 60 meters deep into the sanctuary and lights up the

Ordinary worshippers did not have the right to enter the sanctuary of the "holy of the holies" of the temples. In the one above, a tabernacle encloses the statue of the god. The priest is placing offerings at the feet of the statue as he says his prayers.

statues of the king and the gods. At right is a cross section of a New Kingdom temple: 1) row of sphinxes, entrance, pylons; 2) court; 3) hypostyle hall; 4) sacred barge chamber; 5) sanctuary of the holy of holies; 6, 7) annexes and storerooms.

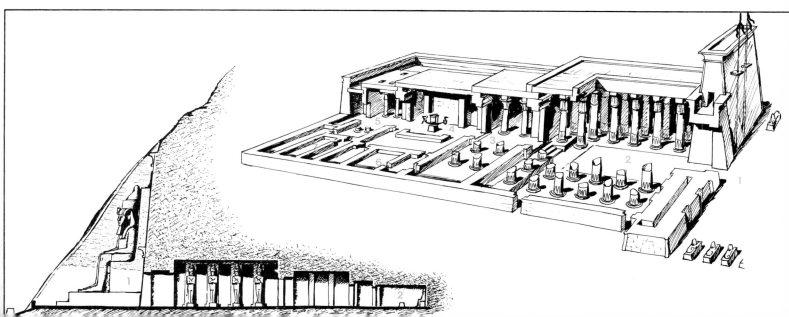

Abode of the dead

The Egyptians believed in the survival of the soul and the body. Everyone possessed not only his "ba," or soul, which embodied his moral and intellectual qualities; but also his "ka," his spiritual self. If, after death, care was not taken of the mummified body, the ka would disappear, because it had to be nourished with care in order to conserve its vital force.

The pharaohs, the noblemen, and the wealthy spent fortunes on burials which would conform to their beliefs. Their corpses were carefully mummified, wrapped in fine bandages, and enclosed in luxurious sarcophagi. The face of the dead person was sculpted on the stone or wood cover, which might be covered with gold.

Inside the sarcophagi were placed papyrus scrolls inscribed with magic formulas that helped the deceased to overcome all obstacles which might keep them from eternal repose. These formulas made up the *Book of the Dead*.

After the corpse had been been mummified, the ceremony of the "opening of the mouth" was performed. This ritual, along with the recitation of magic words, was supposed to give life back to the deceased and symbolized the return of the ka into his body. This rite was performed once again on the day of the funeral. The funeral chamber was supplied with all that might be needed to permit the body to survive—food, drink, beds and benches, and little statues that were to act as servants. The chamber of Tutankhamen contained beds for resting and for decoration, a complete set of furniture, dishes of gold, chariots, and even boats!

The pharaoh's subjects were obliged to bring offerings to him; and in front of the private tombs or in the mastabas, rectangular tombs of the Old Kingdom, there was an altar to receive the poultry, meats, wheat, and fruits that the deceased would need. But offerings were placed even on the humble graves of the poor, dug in the desert and marked by a simple stone. Indeed, the religion of the dead made the poor as well as the powerful equal before the divine judgment.

During the rite of the "opening of the mouth" a priest reads magic formulas.

The poor were buried in the sand, wrapped in a straw mat as above. A square hole was dug and the arms and legs of the corpse folded so that it lay on its side. In order to keep the jackals from digging up the body, a heavy stone was placed over the grave.

Under the Old Kingdom, rich Egyptians had their tombs or mastabas built of brick. Their statue-portraits stood in a walled chamber, the "serdab" (left). The narrow opening was supposed to enable the statue of the deceased to attend ceremonies and accept offerings.

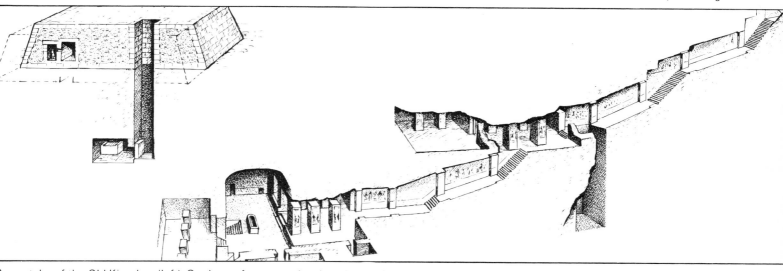

A mastaba of the Old Kingdom (left). On the surface were the chapel and the chamber containing the statue of the dead. The corpse was buried in the underground vault by means of a shaft. A royal tomb at Thebes (right) was entered from the mountain. A shaft dug under the

first gallery was meant to deter plunderers and to drain off infiltrating water. The funerary chamber with the sarcophagus was situated at the farther end of the gallery.

Mummified corpses were placed in richly decorated sarcophagi. The sarcophagus above has been placed on a sleigh-shaped barge on runners and is being pulled over the sand by oxen. Mourners follow the procession to the tomb dug into a cliff.

To embalm the dead, the brain and viscera were removed and the body washed and covered with salts for many days to dry it. The cavities were cleaned and filled with spices. Then the body was wrapped in bandages of linen soaked in aromatic gums.

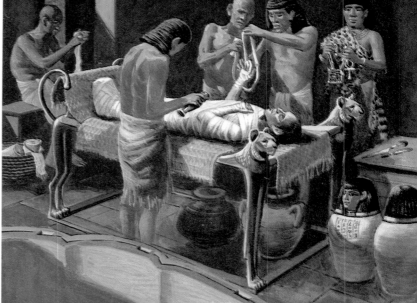

1. The infant sun emerging from a lotus
2. Ra, the sun god. United with Amon into a composite personage, he was the most important dynastic divinity of Egypt.
3. The goddess Nut personified the arc of the sky. Her body, spanning the heavens, was spangled with stars. During the day Ra, the sun god, traversed this heavenly arc, but at night, Nut returned to her husband, the earth, and darkness descended.
4. Baboon god watches over the journey of the sun barge, 5.
6. Isis, wife of Osiris, mother of Horus
7. Nephthys, sister of Osiris and wife of Seth
8. Maat, goddess of justice, who symbolizes the divine order
9. Horus, falcon-god, son of Osiris
10. Osiris in mummified form. He was the god of fertility and of the lower regions.

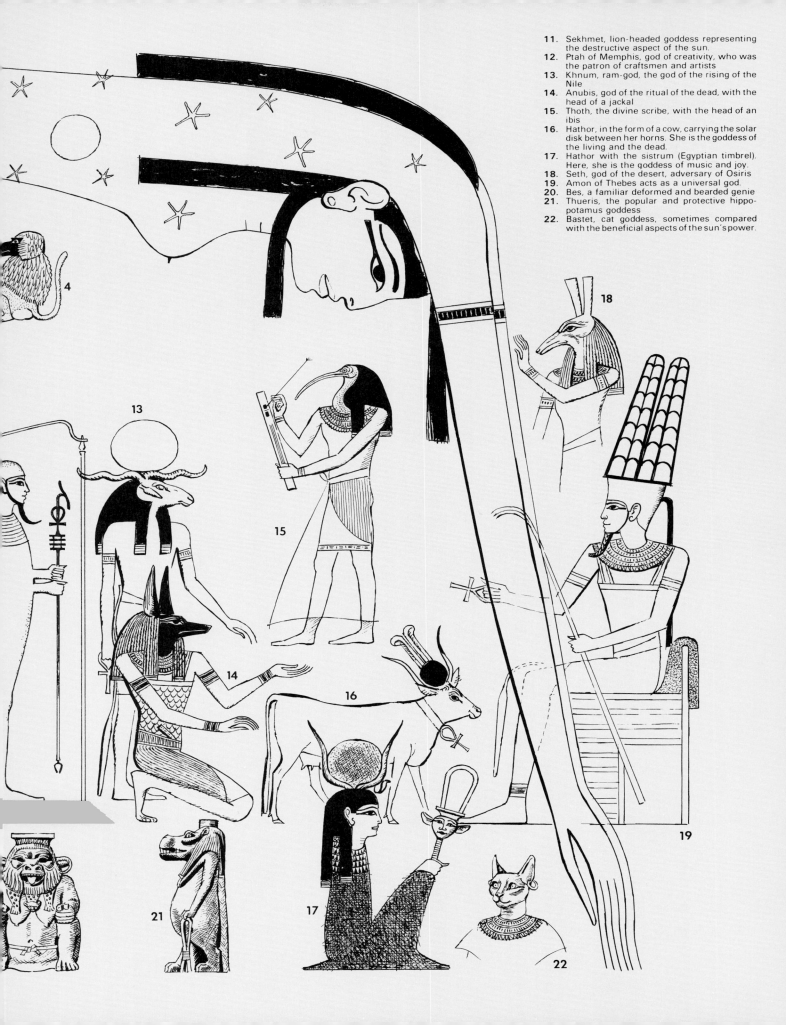

11. Sekhmet, lion-headed goddess representing the destructive aspect of the sun.
12. Ptah of Memphis, god of creativity, who was the patron of craftsmen and artists
13. Khnum, ram-god, the god of the rising of the Nile
14. Anubis, god of the ritual of the dead, with the head of a jackal
15. Thoth, the divine scribe, with the head of an ibis
16. Hathor, in the form of a cow, carrying the solar disk between her horns. She is the goddess of the living and the dead.
17. Hathor with the sistrum (Egyptian timbrel). Here, she is the goddess of music and joy.
18. Seth, god of the desert, adversary of Osiris
19. Amon of Thebes acts as a universal god.
20. Bes, a familiar deformed and bearded genie
21. Thueris, the popular and protective hippopotamus goddess
22. Bastet, cat goddess, sometimes compared with the beneficial aspects of the sun's power.

The Bestiary of the Pharaohs

The animals that lived in the times of the pharaohs are probably the most perfectly documented in all of ancient history. Many of them were adored as divinities, and many were used as hieroglyphic symbols. There exists a wealth of figurines, statues, and frescoes representing animals of all sorts which were faithfully reproduced by the artists of the era and later found in the tombs of the pharaohs.

FROM ANIMAL-GODS TO ANIMALIZED GODS

Adoration of animals and nature are found over and over again in the spiritual views of societies in which man has felt himself dominated by the forces in his environment. Not only the beasts, but the sun, earth, water, moon, sky, and death all represent mysterious forces which are certainly feared, but at the same time admired and revered for their beneficial influences or for the strength they embodied. Thus man might respect the ferociousness of the lion, the strength of the crocodile, or the care of the cow for its calf.

In the religion of the ancient Egyptians, the gods were at first represented in very realistic animal form. Then, gradually, the divinities began to take on human form, with only the head preserving animal characteristics; or, sometimes, merely one single animal attribute—horns, for example, was kept. It can be assumed that these gods represented animals that were at one time very abundant in Egypt, but that in some cases have since disappeared.

Anubis, god of the dead, had the characteristics of a jackal; Khnum, the prolific creator, was represented by a ram; Thoth, the god of wisdom, was sometimes symbolized by an ibis and sometimes by a baboon. Hathor, goddess of love and birth, had the appearance of a cow; whereas Sekhmet resembled a lioness. Thueris, who assured fertility and birth, had the body of a hippopotamus; and Apis, also a god of fruitfulness, took the form of a bull. Horus, the god of the sky, with his falcon head, became the protector of the pharaoh. Other popular animals, such as beetles and vultures, also played a role in Egyptian mythology. All these gods maintained complicated influences over the events of life on earth, the movements of the stars, and passage into the hereafter. To these very numerous gods were also added the demigods. And the kings who represented these divinities became godlike themselves, with their semi-divine, semi-royal emblems, such as the crown of the ram or Uraeus, the cobra.

BREEDS OF DOGS

Dogs held an important place among the domesticated animals. Although the Egyptians sometimes placed them in the sarcophagi, they did not seem to show them much affection. No scenes exist showing them playing with these animals or petting them. One of the most popular breeds was a kind of greyhound, ancestor of the modern saluki. Standing on long legs, it had a long, hairy tail, an elongated snout, and floppy ears. There was also another breed of dog which was short-haired and had long, pointed ears which stood straight up. It is possible that Anubis, the jackal god, was a representation of these dogs. Both breeds had narrow chests, and tails which curled up. Some mummies of a smaller species of greyhound, called *ketket*, have been found in the tombs of women, accompanied by mummified dwarfs. The princes considered these animals most prestigious, and dressed them in gold leather collars decorated with flowers. They gave them such names as "White Gazelle" or "Master" to show their pride in possessing such fine animals.

Another type of dog, doubtlessly introduced by the Hyksos, resembled our modern mastiff.

A modern but rare breed, which came from the Balearic Islands and was called "dog of the pharaohs," was used about a century ago in Spain for hunting wolves. It was called *podenco ibicenco*, and it must have been introduced on the little island of Ibiza by the Phoenecians. This large, slender dog with powerful jaws strongly resembled the painted wooden Anubis that was found in the tomb of Tutankhamen in Thebes. Perhaps this god of the dead was not a jackal (an animal which paradoxically has the reputation of digging up human bones in the cemeteries), but the ancestor of the *podenco*, this dog, with upright ears, sometimes called the "pharaohs' greyhound." It must be noted that the podenco was not a greyhound, but a different kind of racing dog, muscular, swift, and gifted with an excellent sense of smell, a characteristic which the greyhound lacks.

P. H. Plantain

A. Vigneau-Tel

MONKEYS AND GEESE

Monkeys lived in the houses of princes and kings, who, it seems, favored them more than dogs. Doubtless this was because monkeys were sacred animals, represented by Thoth, the god of wisdom. They were never punished for the damage that they did in the orchards and gardens. The same was true of the geese of the Nile, for the goose was not considered a barnyard fowl but a pet animal, free to wander through the house. It was not even sacrificed to the gods. It is possible that the *Smon*, the Nile goose, was considered a sort of "watchdog," such as the famous Geese of the Capitol, found much later in Rome.

Giraudon

AN EGYPTIAN BOARD GAME

The Egyptians spent a good part of their leisure time playing a popular game called *mehen,* or the "serpent game." This game was very much like many of our popular board games, such as parcheesi or the French "goose game." It was played on a little table on which was carved a coiled snake, with its head in the center, and its body divided into sections. It is not known exactly how the game was played or what the rules were, but we do know that the players had three lions and three lionesses and little white and red balls, often made of ivory, which were kept in a little ebony box. The Egyptians were very fond of games. Some of the games also had a social role in that they sometimes helped players forget their quarrels.

A SACRED CAT OF MYSTERIOUS ORIGINS

Bulloz

The lioness Sekhmet, goddess of war, was succeeded by another feline divinity, Bastet, the cat-goddess. But there is a question among zoologists as to whether Sekhmet was indeed a lioness and Bastet a cat. Indeed, some experts see more of the characteristics of a panther or a cheetah in Sekhmet; and in Bastet, a sort of reduced model of both. In any case, cheetahs and panthers, as well as lions, abounded in ancient Egypt. In mythology, the panther represented the sky; a cape of a panther's skin was a symbol of royalty, and there are two statues of Tutankhamen in which the pharaoh, with a scepter and whip in his hand, is standing on a black panther. As for the goddess Bastet, her appearance and her suppleness resemble more those of a prestigious feline than those of an ordinary cat. There is no evidence that she had anything in common with the cats of today. She more closely resembled the *Felis chaus,* a species of cat which is found today mainly in Egypt, where it lives in the marshy thickets and reed beds.

Since about 2500 B.C., these "cats" appeared in the temple, where they replaced the tame lions as guardians. They were also to be found in the homes of Egyptian families, along with statuettes of Bastet.

Many Egyptians believed that the cat was their ancestor. The women used makeup to give themselves a cat-like look, and children were consecrated to Bastet by making a cut in an arm, into which a priest poured several drops of cat's blood. When a cat died, the sorrow of its masters was so great that they shaved off their eyebrows as a sign of mourning. It is believed that the breed of cat pictured below is the descendant of the cats of ancient Egypt.

P. H. Plantain

HUNTING IN THE MARSHLANDS

Because it was so prolific, the cat symbolized the fertility of the land; and because of its cleanliness, it represented virginity. The cat was not considered a mouse hunter as it is today. In ancient Egypt, it was the mongoose that hunted mice. The Egyptians took their cats with them when they went hunting for waterfowl. This fact has been documented by several frescoes.

One of these in particular, a painting on stucco discovered in the tomb of Nebamon in Thebes, and dating from 1400 B.C., shows the deceased making his way among the reeds aboard a light boat made of papyrus. His wife and child accompany him, along with their cat. The hunter, who has already captured three grey herons, is brandishing a stick which he uses as a thrusting weapon. A pet Nile goose serves as a decoy. Birds and butterflies fly about in all directions. The cat, which has seized two birds, one of which resembles a long-tailed tit, pounces on a female duck

which manages to fly away. Among the aquatic birds which are represented, an opened peacock's tail can be recognized.

Like the fish, the waterfowl, especially the teals and ducks, were also caught in nets. They were lured into the marshland by live decoys to be trapped by the hunters.

HUNTING ON THE PLAIN

Smaller birds, such as orioles and other species which came to visit the gardens and orchards in spring and autumn, were also caught with nets, although spring traps were occasionally used. But it was mostly the children who hunted these birds. Once the birds became entangled in the nets which covered the trees, the children climbed under the nets and seized the birds, which they placed in cages.

Quail of the species *Coturnix coturnix,* a wild bird which has been practically wiped out,[1] were so plentiful in ancient Egypt that at the time of their migrations, they created clouds large enough to block the sun. Exhausted by their journey, the birds fell to the ground. Hunters, dressed in sandals so as not to cut their feet on the stubble field, easily captured them with small-meshed nets stretched over wooden frames. These frames were placed on the ground. As soon as the birds landed on them, the men pounced, waving big white scarves, and frightening the quail so that they did not even try to fly away. Instead they became entangled in the meshes of the net. These quail were a delicacy, appreciated by princes and peasants; even the gods, or rather their priests, relished them. Amon-Ra was presented with 21,700 of them under the reign of Ramses III, in addition to some 80,000 other birds.

[1] The great migrations of quail continued up to the beginning of the 20th century. At the end of the 19th century, the Egyptians exported more than 2 million birds each year. The record of 3 million was attained in 1920. In about 1930, the massive flights of quail ceased.

THE PRINCES AND KINGS GO HUNTING

Hunting large animals in the desert was mainly the sport of princes. But, in addition to these "amateurs," a corps of "professionals" was instituted by Ramses III. The mission of these especially designated archers was simple—to capture or kill the maximum number of animals, especially gazelles, so that they could be offered to the gods. Other royal officers accompanied them in their work and performed such tasks as gathering up all that was useful, such as huge ostrich eggs and feathers and sweet wild honey.

Neither the hunts of the noblemen nor those of the pharaoh's professionals were very heroic, however, in spite of the magnificent spectacle which marked their end. Indeed, rarely did a hunter go out into the desert alone, mounted on a swift chariot and accompanied by his greyhounds. The method that was used was much less dangerous. Water and food were placed in a narrow valley, the sides and back of which could be closed off by nets, if necessary. Rabbits, gazelles, buffalo, ibexes, hyenas, and ostriches would gather in the valley. When the men arrived with their servants and dogs, the massacre would begin! Arrows would rain down from all sides; the mastiffs and greyhounds would round up all the animals that were hopelessly trying to escape. The return from this kind of hunt was a parade of gasping animals, heads hung low, four legs tied to a pole which was carried by two men.

The catches were impressive: 54 oryx, 1 hartebeest, 81 gazelles; another time, 367 oryx, 20,000 buffalo. And these figures represent only a portion of the offerings made to Amon during the reign of Ramses III!

The pharaoh himself did not take part in these bloody adventures. To assure his prestige and his reputation of invincibility, he hunted the biggest and most dangerous animals so that the scribes could sing his praises as they recounted his feats. But these large species did not exist in the desert bordering on the Nile, so he had to go farther, beyond the falls which crossed the Egyptian river farther south. The adversaries which he went after were, of course, lions, and perhaps elephants.

These he pursued mounted on his chariot with a bow and a spear as his only weapons, so that one day it could be told in the paintings that would adorn his tomb: "Never had a king accomplished such a feat since the time of the god. . . ."

UNDER THE SIGN
OF THE BULL

Contrary to popular belief, the Egyptians did not worship just one single bull. Rather, Egyptians in the time of the pharaohs gave their devotion to three bulls chosen only because of the particular coloration of their hides: Buchis, an animal which was entirely white with a black head; Mnevis, with a black coat sprinkled with spots shaped like ears of corn; Apis, the most renowned, also black but distinctive because of two white spots of a very special and definite shape—one a triangle on the forehead, the other, on the back, a crescent, or a shape resembling a bird of prey with outstretched wings. When one of the bull-gods died, its replacement inevitably became a problem. Therefore, after it was embalmed, it was placed in an elaborate sarcophagus, and once the required seventy days of mourning had passed, the priests undertook the task of finding a successor with the same markings and coloration as the dead bull-god. When such a successor was found, it was kept penned up for fourteen days. Only the priests could come near it to feed it, although women could look at it. These bulls were chosen from a breed of animals with horns which stood upright, generally in the shape of a lyre. This characteristic added to their majestic bearing. The Egyptians raised several varieties of cattle which they called by different names, but it is unclear whether these names indicated breed or weight.

The cattle were raised to serve several important purposes—for their milk and its by-products, to be harnessed to chariots and plows, and for their meat.

The oiua, an African animal with long horns, was carefully fattened until it became so enormous that it could no longer walk. The oundjou belonged to a smaller breed with very small horns, and sometimes none at all. The nega was a fiercer animal, but large in size, with ample horns.

ANIMALS FOR BREEDING

It was the Egyptians who first attempted to domesticate all sorts of animals, some with success that has lasted up to our day, and others which they were forced to abandon. Among the latter were hyenas and a breed of wolf which they tried with little success to train for hunting.

Along with the oxen, donkeys were raised to carry burdens. Pigs, goats, and lambs were also raised. It is not certain whether their flesh was eaten, because male goats were worshipped at Mendes, as was the ram-god Harsaphes. As for the donkeys, they were considered impure animals as were, probably, pigs. Pigs and lambs were used to trample seeds into fields which had been flooded and were ready for planting. Among the wild species which the Egyptians undertook to tame in order to offer them to the gods were various antelopes, such as hartebeests, oryxes, and addaxes. These were kept in stables at night and were let out into an enclosure during the day. Roosters and chickens were not yet known. They would be introduced in the

Giraudon

6th and 5th centuries B.C. However, in the barnyards, which always had a body of water in the center, many web-footed birds were kept. There were all kinds of ducks, descendants of birds captured alive in the swamps. There were at least two species of geese different from the Nile goose, as well as pelicans and several kinds of cranes.

For a thousand years, the Egyptians had domesticated pigeons. They were the first to use them as "travelers," releasing them from their boats during the invasions of the "People of the Sea."

There were tens of thousands of them kept in pigeon houses. However, pigeons were also eaten, along with quail, various waterfowl, and beef. Paradoxically, in this country where fertility depended on the presence of the Nile, the eating of fish was considered an abomination by the princes and kings. In spite of laws which periodically went so far as to forbid the use of this food, the ordinary people did not deprive themselves of it nor did, it seems, those whose duty it was to service the temples, for 441,000 fish were found among the offerings made at Thebes and Memphis. Some of these fish were so heavy that it took two men to carry them.

Hassia

AN ADVANTAGEOUS DEFEAT

In about 1700 B.C., the Hyksos crossed Syria and invaded Egypt, which they occupied for more than a century. Finally the Egyptian king, Kamose, succeeded around 1580 in pushing them back beyond his frontiers. These conquerors were far from having attained the degree of civilization of the conquered, but their presence was nevertheless beneficial for Egypt, for they introduced horses into the country. These animals were little known, and certainly the Egyptians did not know how to use them until the Hyksos invasion. According to what can be determined, this horse, which the Egyptians called "The Beautiful," was not a model species. Large, with a shortened head; thin, with a narrow rump and shoulders; it was very often represented by the artists of the time with a sway back, an elaborate headdress, and rearing up on very long legs. Later this animal took a favored place in religious ceremonies. A painting shows it mounted by Horus, the falcon-god, who is piercing Sebek, the crocodile-god, with his lance.

This new acquisition greatly changed the military organization of the pharaohs, and made the Egyptians mounted raiders who periodically invaded that part of the world during the following centuries.

The Egyptians harnessed their war horses to light chariots, a technique which they also learned from their conquerors. The Egyptian war chariots held two men—a driver who wielded the whip and a soldier who used a bow and arrows and javelins. A fresco shows Ramses III in a great battle against the Libyans. The pharaoh is shown alone in his chariot, the reins of his horse attached to his belt so that he can bend his bow. Was this an exception granted as a royal prerogative? It is more likely that the artist wished in this way to magnify even more the extraordinary feat of the king. Behind him, there is shown a second person, probably an officer whose duty it was to carry the golden carafe and goblet to quench Ramses' thirst during the battle.

Large numbers of these chariots were used in combat. In 1250 B.C., Ramses II used 3,500 at a time in one battle. From that date, great progress was made in Egypt in the breeding of horses. The pharaohs had stallions brought from Syria and used them as stud horses in Memphis and in Thebes, and even exported their offspring.

The Arabian horse introduced by the Hyksos became the ancestor of the Dongola, a modern horse of the Upper Nile, now found in Eritrea, Abyssinia, and Nubia. The Barb, a horse of northern Africa, is also descended from the original horses of the Hyksos.

Glossary

Acacia A thorny tree with white or yellow flowers

Alabaster A whitish translucent stone used for carving

Amulet An ornament worn as a charm against evil

Aswan An ancient city near the first cataract of the Nile

Book of the Dead Papyrus scrolls with magic formulas entombed with the dead to help them in their next life

Carnelian A red or reddish-brown stone used in jewelry

Cataract A large waterfall

Crane A tall, long-legged wading bird

Crook A hooked or curved stick

Delta The triangular island sometimes found at the mouth of a river

Embalm To treat a body so it will not decay

Faience Highly colored glazed pottery

Flail Two wooden sticks joined by a thong, used for threshing grain

Fresco A painting made on new plaster before it dries

Hathoric column An Egyptian column with the top carved to resemble the goddess Hathor

Hieroglyphics Pictures or symbols used by the Egyptians to stand for ideas, words, or sounds

Hypostyle hall A hall built so that the roof rests on rows of columns

Jackal A wild dog

Ketket A kind of greyhound

Lapis lazuli A bright blue stone used in jewelry

Lotus A kind of water lily often shown in Egyptian art

Lower Egypt The part of ancient Egypt in the north, near the mouth of the Nile

Mastaba A rectangular room in a tomb, connected to the mummy chamber

Mehen An Egyptian board game

Memphis An important city in Lower Egypt, near the Nile delta

Mummify To treat a body with preservatives, so that it will not decay

Obelisk A four-sided pillar, often made from a single piece of stone

Papyrus A tall grasslike plant that grows along the banks of the Nile

Pharaoh The title of the rulers of ancient Egypt

Pomegranate A red fruit with many seeds

Protodoric column An early, very simple style of column design

Pylon The large flat-topped stone monument at each side of the entrance to a temple or tomb

Pyramid A large monument with triangular sides meeting at a point at the top; used as tombs for the pharaohs

Relief Carving in which the subject is raised from the background

Sarcophagus A stone coffin, often carved or decorated

Savannah A grassy treeless plain

Scribe In ancient Egypt, a person who earned a living by reading, writing, and keeping records

Senit An Egyptian game like backgammon or checkers

Serdab A small room in a tomb containing a statue of the dead person

Sestrum An Egyptian timbrel; a small hand drum or tambourine

Shaduf A balance system used to raise water in a bucket to irrigate crops

Sheaf A bundle of stalks of grain or straw

Smon A Nile goose

Sphinx A large statue with the body of a lion and the head of a man, ram, or hawk

Stucco A plasterlike material used to cover walls

Tabernacle A tent or shelter that contains religious objects

Thebes An important city on the Nile in Upper Egypt

Timbrel A small hand drum or tambourine

Turquoise A blue-green stone used in jewelry

Unguent A salve or ointment

Upper Egypt The part of ancient Egypt in the south, along the upper Nile

Uraeus The image of a sacred form used on the headdress of Egyptian rulers

Vizier An important official, chief minister of the pharaoh

Zither A stringed instrument played with a pick or the fingers

Index